Discover! 3

Sound And Music

Richard Northcott

Contents

OXFORD
UNIVERSITY PRESS

OXFORD

UNIVERSITY PRESS

Great Clarendon Street, Oxford OX2 6DP

Oxford University Press is a department of the University of Oxford. It furthers the University's objective of excellence in research, scholarship, and education by publishing worldwide in

Oxford New York

Auckland Cape Town Dar es Salaam Hong Kong Karachi Kuala Lumpur Madrid Melbourne Mexico City Nairobi New Delhi Shanghai Taipei Toronto

With offices in

Argentina Austria Brazil Chile Czech Republic France Greece Guatemala Hungary Italy Japan Poland Portugal Singapore South Korea Switzerland Thailand Turkey Ukraine Vietnam

OXFORD and OXFORD ENGLISH are registered trade marks of Oxford University Press in the UK and in certain other countries

© Oxford University Press 2011

The moral rights of the author have been asserted

Database right Oxford University Press (maker)

First published 2011

2015 2014 2013 2012 2011

10 9 8 7 6 5 4 3 2

No unauthorized photocopying

All rights reserved. No part of this publication may be reproduced, stored in a retrieval system, or transmitted, in any form or by any means, without the prior permission in writing of Oxford University Press, or as expressly permitted by law, or under terms agreed with the appropriate reprographics rights organization. Enquiries concerning reproduction outside the scope of the above should be sent to the ELT Rights Department, Oxford University Press, at the address above

You must not circulate this book in any other binding or cover and you must impose this same condition on any acquirer

Any websites referred to in this publication are in the public domain and their addresses are provided by Oxford University Press for information only. Oxford University Press disclaims any responsibility for the content

ISBN: 978 0 19 464384 9

An Audio CD Pack containing this book and a CD is also available, ISBN 978 0 19 464424 2

The CD has a choice of American and British English recordings of the complete text.

An accompanying Activity Book is also available, ISBN 978 0 19 464394 8

Printed in China

This book is printed on paper from certified and well-managed sources.

ACKNOWLEDGEMENTS

Illustrations by: Alan Rowe pp.24, 30, 34, 41, 42, 46, 47; Kelly Kennedy pp.4, 19, 22; Ian Moores pp.5, 7, 8, 15, 28; Dusan Pavlic/Beehive Illustration pp.24, 30, 34, 38, 42, 46, 47.

The Publishers would also like to thank the following for their kind permission to reproduce photographs and other copyright material: Alamy p.4 (Andrew Fox), 7 (Fine Art Commercial/baby), 9 (Tarek El Juan/singing lesson), 12 (Peter Horree/gamelan, GM Photo Images, tango band), 13 (Klaus-Werner Friedrich/koto player), 15 (The Print Collector), 16 (Gianni Muratore), 21 (Eddie Gerald/gramophone), 22 (Tim Cuff); Corbis pp.9 (© ILYA NAYMUSHIN/Reuters/throat singer), 13 (© Frédéric Soltan/Sygma/sitar player), 14 (© Jacques Sarrat/Sygma), 17 (© Andy Rain/epa/band); Getty Images pp.7 (David Frazier/Stone/truck), 17 (altrendo images/flamenco), 20 (Ryan McVay/Stone), 23 (Matt Gray/Stone); Oxford University Press pp.3, 10, 11, 18, 19, 21 (cassettes and cds); Photolibrary pp.6 (David Deas), 21 (Eric Nathan/Britain on View/jukebox).

With thanks to Mary Colson for checking music content

Introduction

Listen to the sounds around you. What can you hear? Can you hear cars? Can you hear people's voices? Maybe you can hear a television, or music on the radio.

Look at these pictures. What are these sounds?
Do you like these sounds?
Which sounds are music?
What type of music do you like?

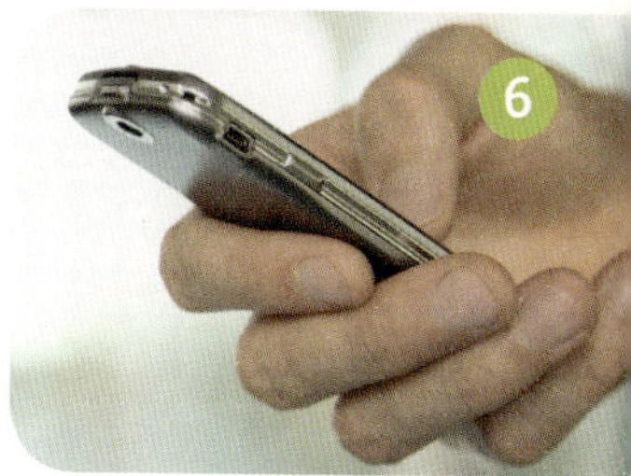

Now read and discover more about sound and music!

How Sound Moves

When you speak, sing, or shout, the sound of your voice moves through the air. The sound goes to other people, and they hear it. Sound moves very fast.

Discover!

Sound moves through air at about 350 meters per second. The sound of a bus moves faster than the bus!

How does sound move through the air?
The air is made of billions of molecules.
The molecules are very small, so you can't
see them.

Your voice pushes the molecules. The
molecules move like waves in the ocean.
The movements of the molecules are
called sound waves.

The sound waves from loud sounds go
far. The sound waves from quiet sounds
don't go far.

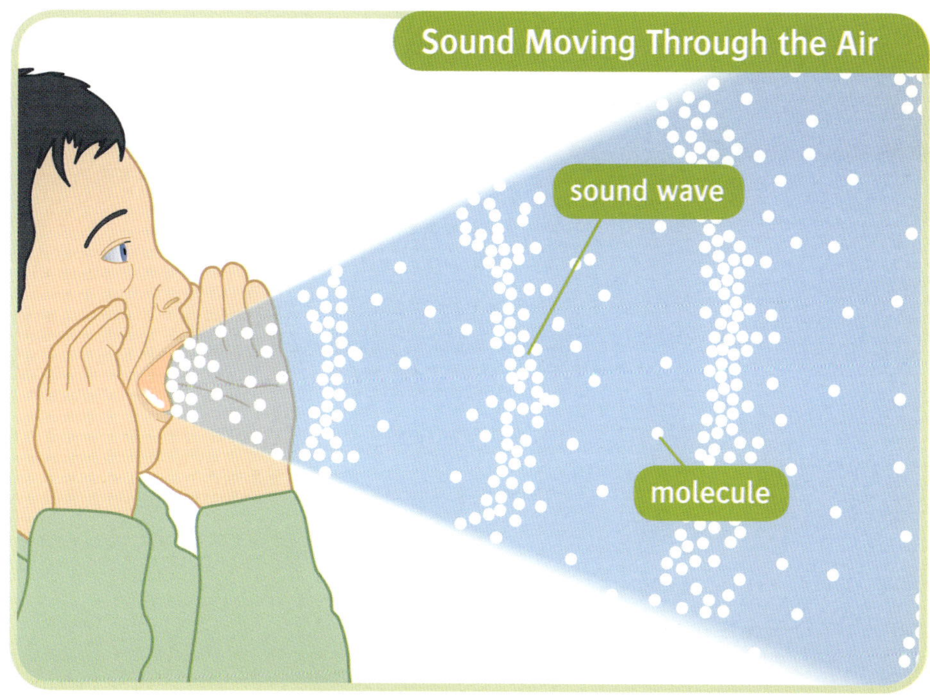

Go to pages 24–25 for activities.

Low Sounds, High Sounds

Some sounds are low and some sounds are high. We can hear low sounds and high sounds everywhere. A plane makes a low sound, but when birds sing, they make a high sound.

Think about the strings of a guitar. The thin strings make a high sound and the thick strings make a low sound.

A Guitar Player

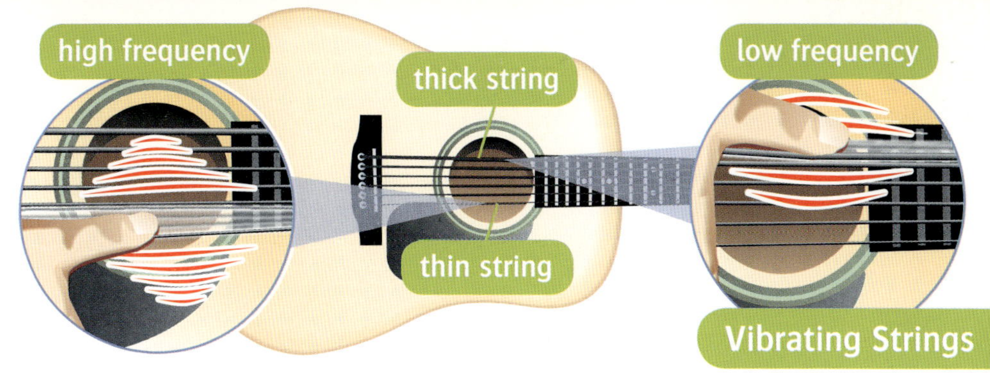

The thin guitar strings vibrate fast. You can't see them move. The thick strings vibrate slowly. These different types of vibration are called frequency. The sound of the thin strings has a high frequency. The sound of the thick strings has a low frequency.

A baby's cry makes a high sound and it has a high frequency. A truck makes a low sound and it has a low frequency. A baby's cry is made of lots of thin sound waves. The sound waves from a truck are thicker.

Go to pages 26–27 for activities.

3 Your Voice

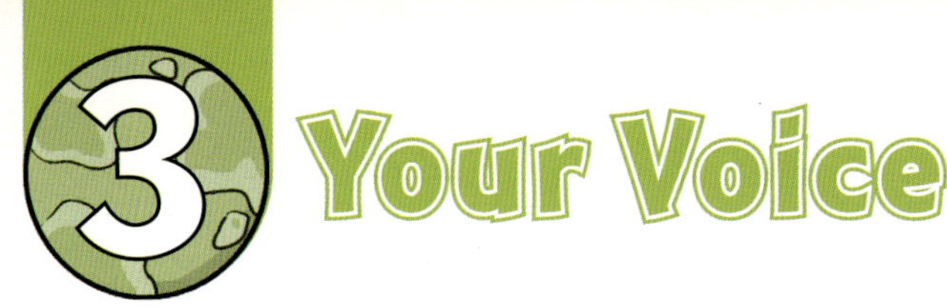

Everyone's voice is different. A man's voice is usually lower than a woman's voice.

Put your hand on the front of your throat and say something. When you speak, your throat vibrates. In your throat, you have vocal cords. When you speak, air from your lungs goes between your vocal cords, and your vocal cords vibrate.

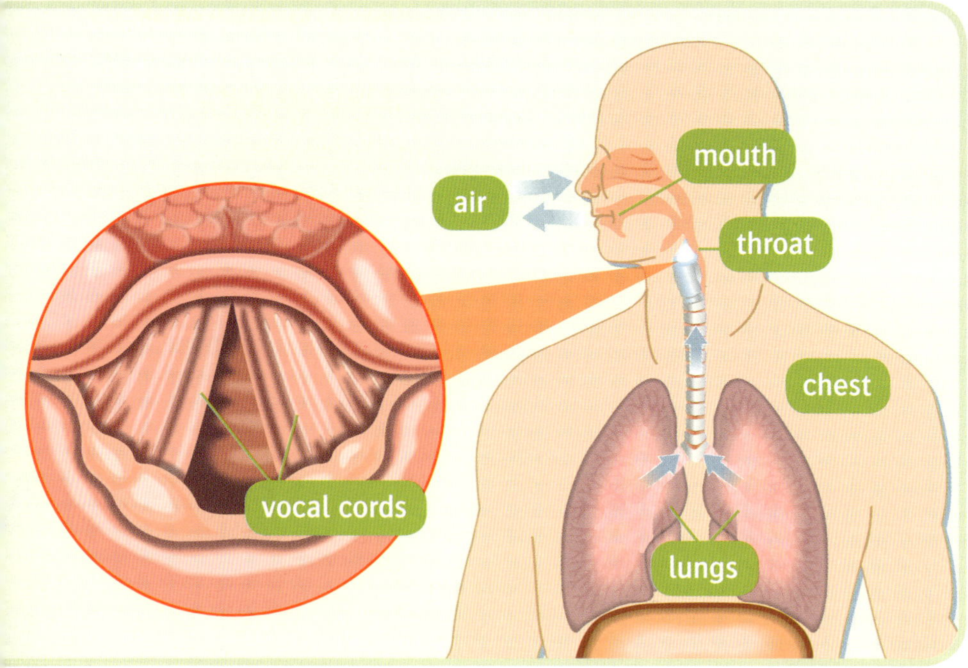

A Singer and Her Teacher

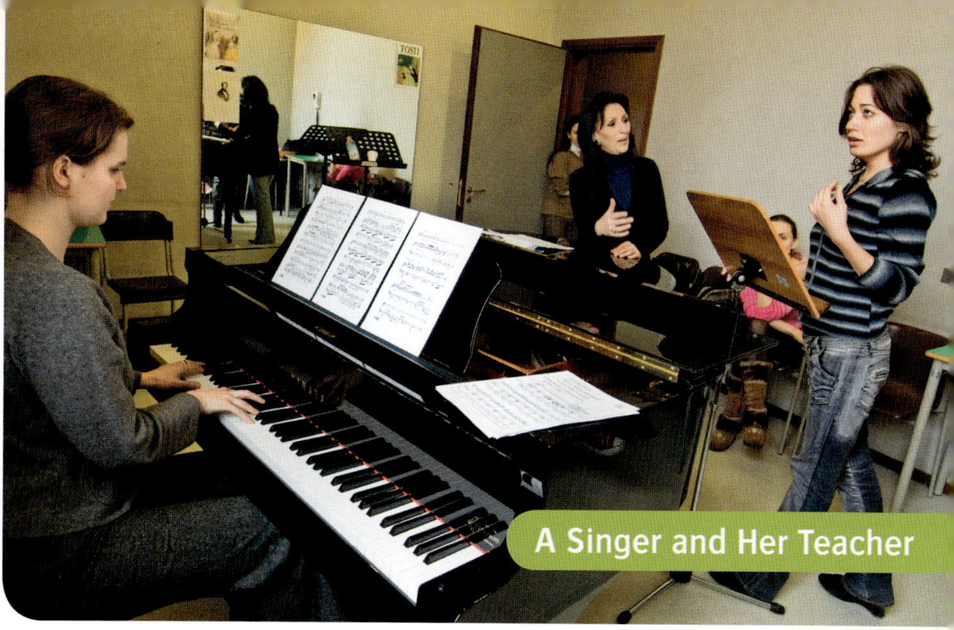

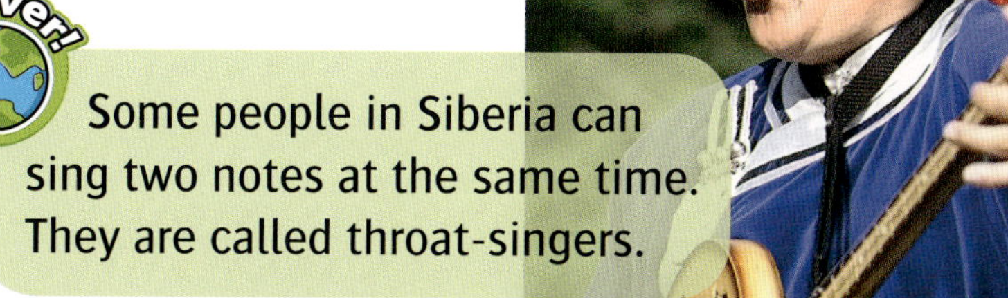

When you sing, you use your mouth, your throat, and your chest. You make your vocal cords shorter or longer, so that you can sing high notes or low notes. Singers can learn how to use their body, so that they can sing better. Some singers have teachers who help them.

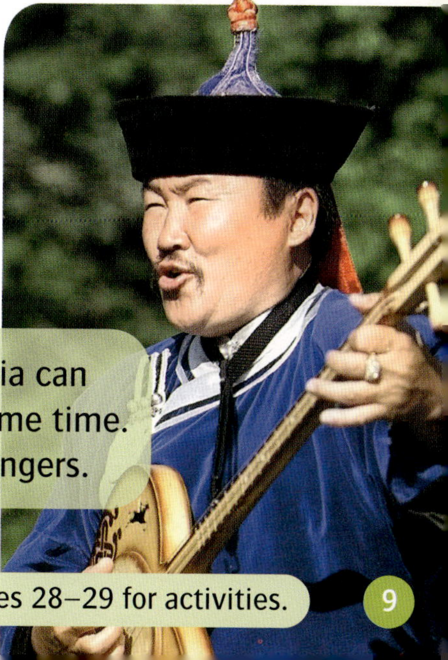

Discover!

Some people in Siberia can sing two notes at the same time. They are called throat-singers.

Go to pages 28–29 for activities.

4 Musical Instruments

Let's look at different musical instruments. Some are called wind instruments. Players use air from their lungs when they play a wind instrument.

Trumpet players press the trumpet on their lips and they blow air into the trumpet. Their lips vibrate, then the air in the trumpet vibrates and makes a sound.

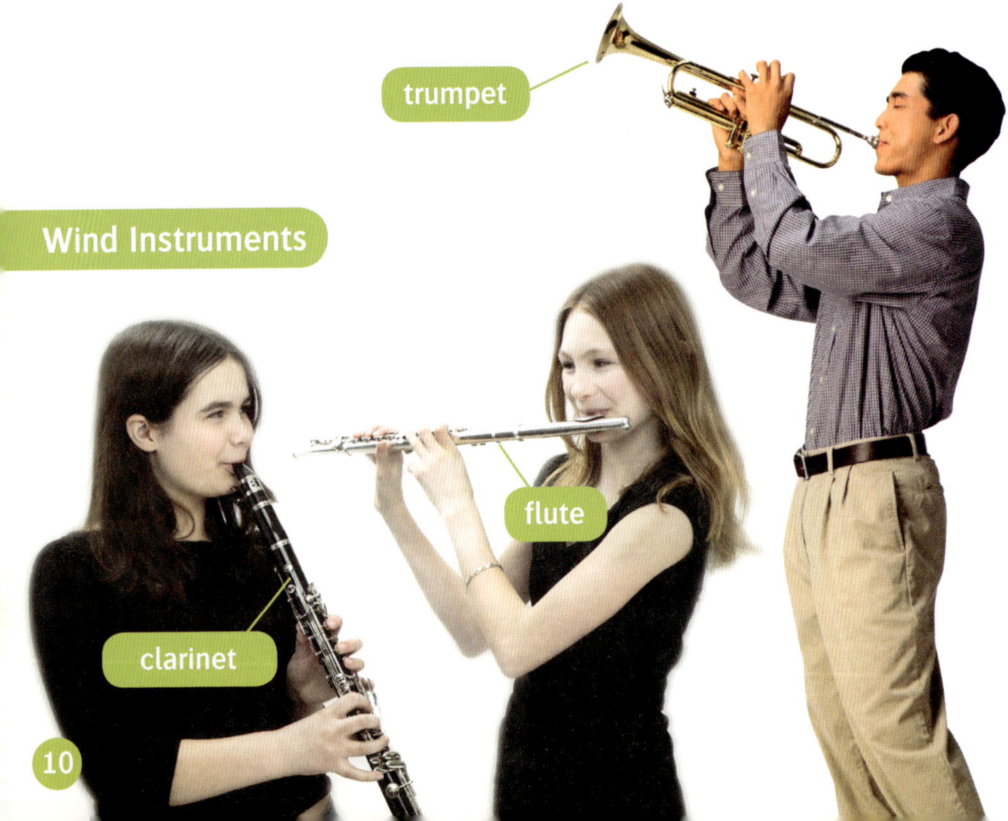

When a drummer hits a drum, the air in the drum vibrates and makes a sound. Other instruments, like cymbals or xylophones, make a sound when the player hits them. These instruments are called percussion instruments.

Guitars, violins, and cellos are stringed instruments. Guitar players pluck the strings of a guitar, but violin and cello players use a bow. They touch the strings with the bow and the strings vibrate.

Go to pages 30–31 for activities.

Around the world you can find thousands of different musical instruments.

In Bali in Indonesia, there are orchestras called gamelans. In a gamelan there are lots of different percussion instruments. The players in a gamelan usually sit on the floor.

The bandoneon is a type of wind instrument. It's like a box with air inside. You squeeze it and it makes a sound. In Argentina, you can listen to bandoneon players in the streets.

A Gamelan in Bali

A Bandoneon Player in Argentina

The koto is a stringed instrument from Japan. It has 13 strings. Koto players pluck the strings with their thumb and two fingers. The players move the small, white bridges to make different notes.

The sitar is a stringed instrument from India. It isn't easy to play. It has lots of strings. Some sitars have 23 strings.

Go to pages 32–33 for activities.

6 Orchestras and Concerts

The musicians in an orchestra listen to their instrument, and to all the other instruments at the same time. The musicians watch their conductor, too.

Musicians in an orchestra always practice before a concert. When they practice, the conductor sometimes tells them to play slower, or more loudly. Conductors move their hands and arms to help the orchestra.

An Orchestra

Different Walls

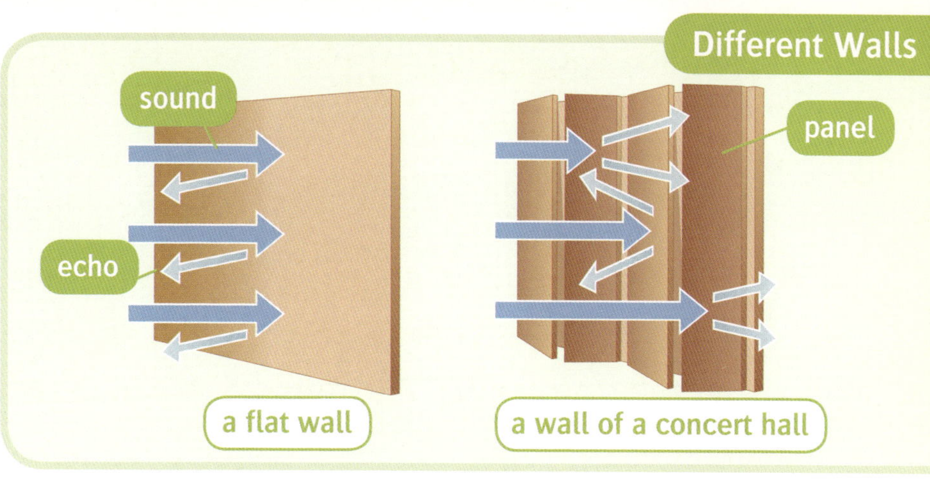

Not all rooms are good for concerts. In a room with flat walls, the sound of the music can bounce off the walls and make an echo. In concert halls, the walls are not flat. They are usually made of different panels. The sound bounces in different ways so there's no echo.

A Painting of Mozart in 1762

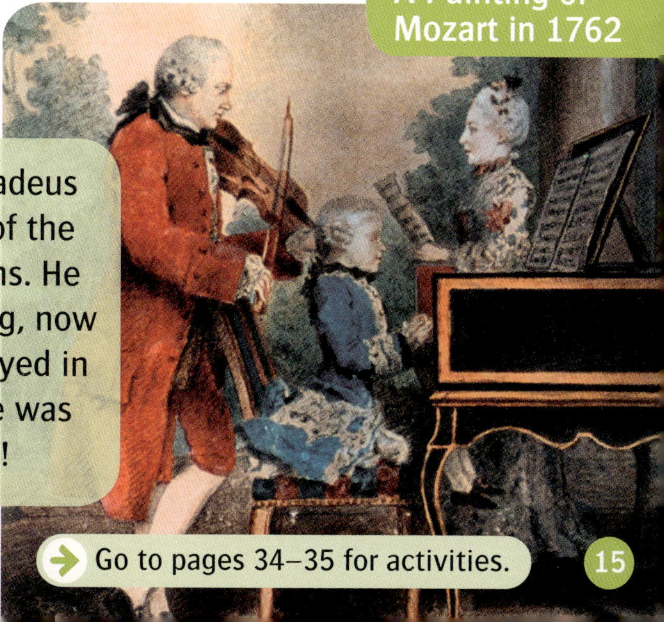

Discover! Wolfgang Amadeus Mozart was one of the greatest musicians. He was from Salzburg, now in Austria. He played in concerts when he was only six years old!

Go to pages 34–35 for activities.

When you listen to music, you sometimes want to tap your foot. When you listen to music with a strong rhythm, you want to dance.

What is rhythm? Sing your favorite song, and tap your foot, too. The sound of your foot is the rhythm of the song. The rhythm of a rock band is strong. When you listen, you want to move or dance.

A Marching Band

A Flamenco Dancer with a Guitar Player

All music has rhythm, but there are different types of rhythm. The rhythm of a marching band is always the same, like the sound of marching.

In flamenco music from Spain, the rhythm gets faster and slower. Flamenco dancing is sometimes slow, and sometimes fast. It's very exciting!

Go to pages 36–37 for activities.

8 Recording Music

Today there's music everywhere. People listen to music at home or in their car. With an MP3 player, they can listen to their favorite songs when they are on a train or walking in the streets.

Where does a song come from? First, a songwriter writes a song and musicians play it. They practice, then they play the song in a recording studio in front of a microphone.

Musicians in a Recording Studio

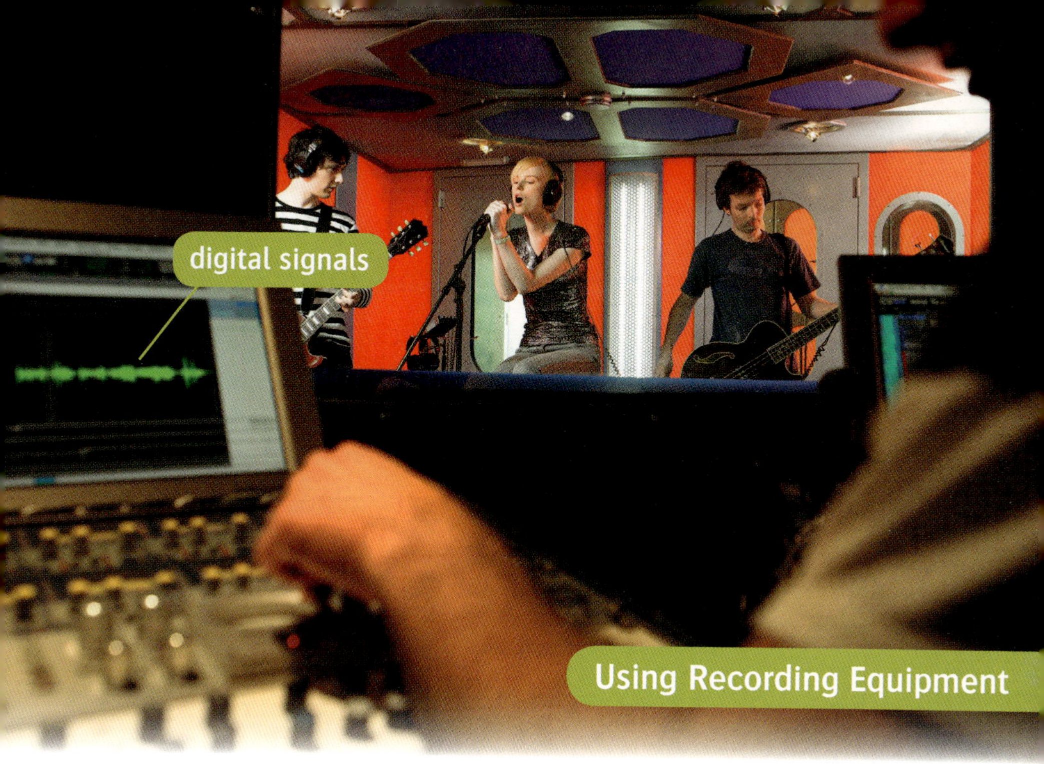

Using Recording Equipment

In the studio, a sound engineer uses recording equipment and records the song. Now the song is a lot of digital signals. The sound engineer uses a computer and works with the signals. This makes the sound of the song better.

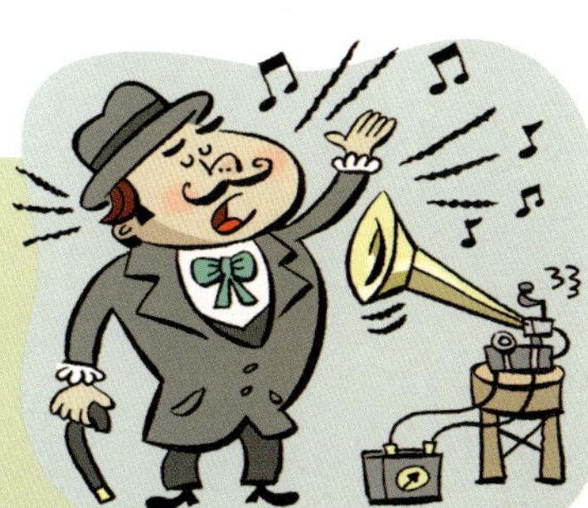

Discover!

The first sound recordings were about 130 years ago. The first microphones were like big trumpets.

Go to pages 38–39 for activities.

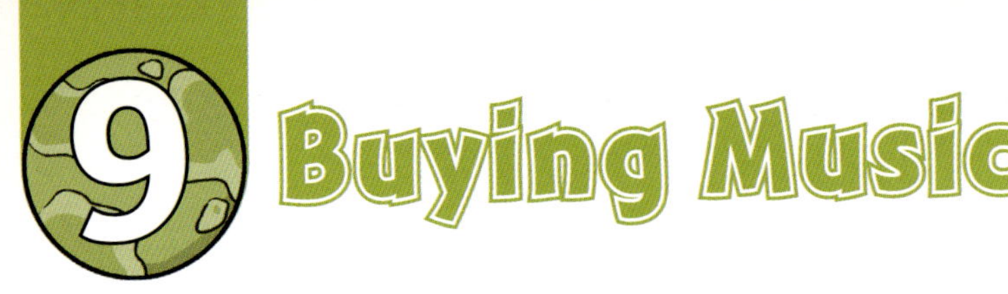

9 Buying Music

Today, people can buy music on the Internet. The music comes to their computer or phone. The music is made of thousands of digital signals. These signals stay on the computer or phone, and people can listen to the music when they want. People can also move the music from their computer to their MP3 player.

Music on the Internet

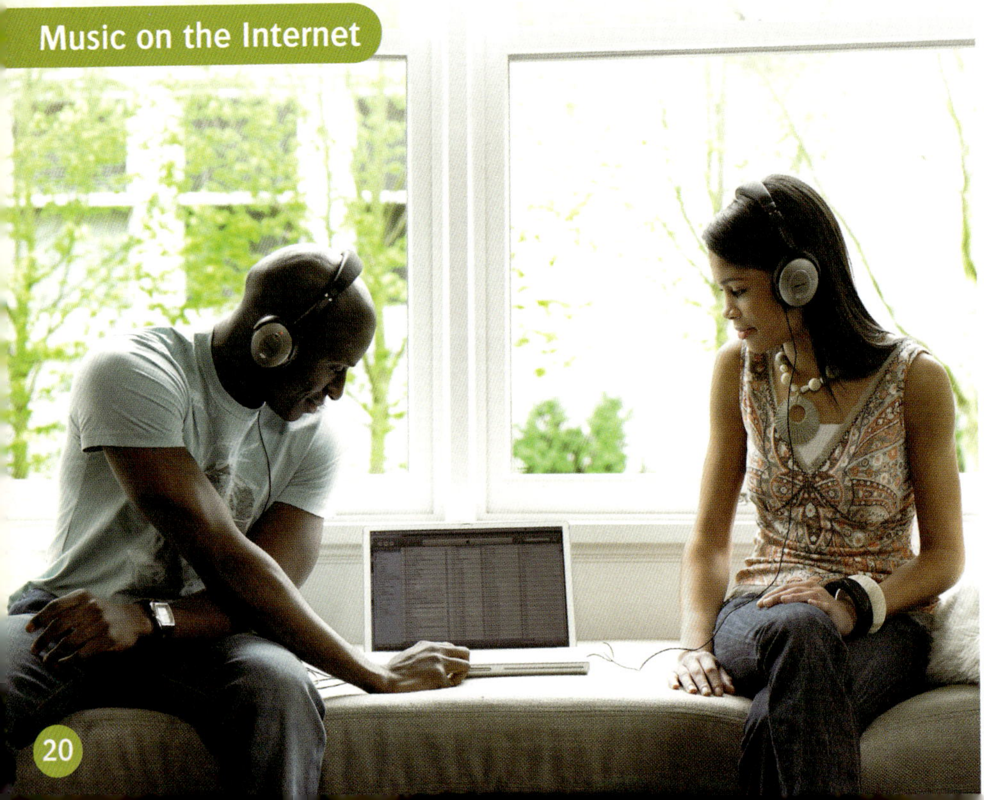

In the past, it wasn't so easy to buy music. About 100 years ago, people started to buy records. They played them on record players. Later, there were big jukeboxes in cafés. In a jukebox there were about 50 records. People put coins in the jukebox and it played their favorite song. About 40 years ago, there were cassettes. They were good because people played them in their cars. Then about 30 years ago, there were compact discs, or CDs.

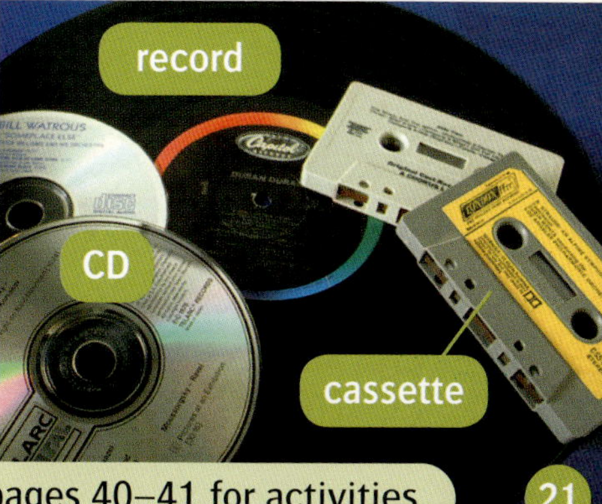

10 Sound and Noise

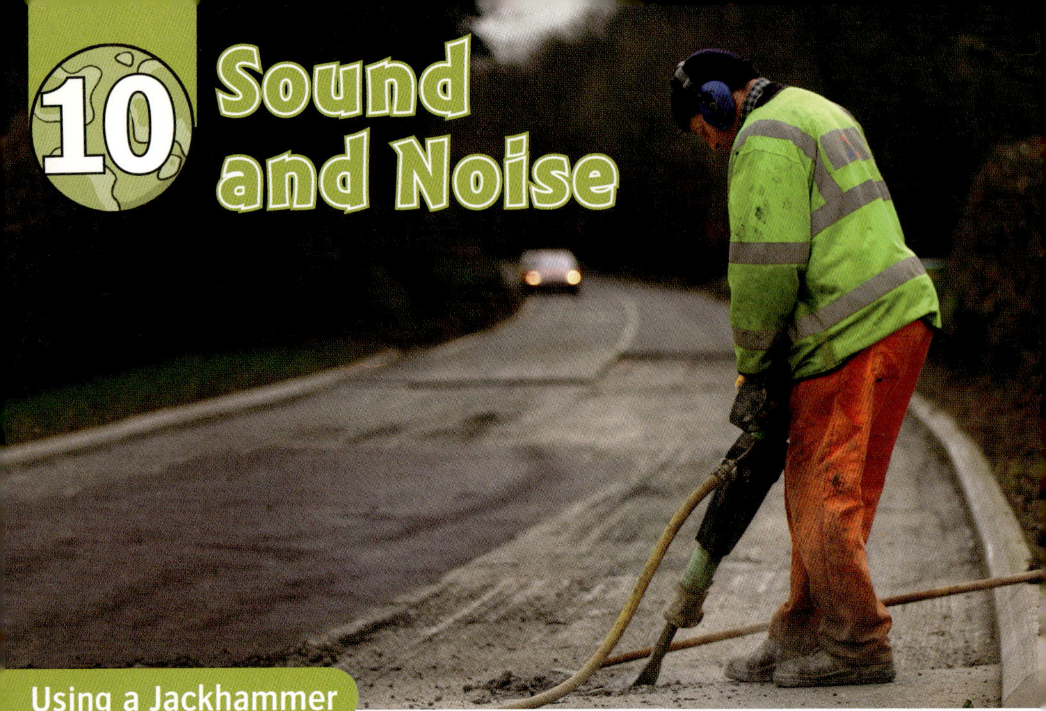

Using a Jackhammer

We measure sound in decibels. The sound of a quiet wind is 10 decibels. When people speak, their voices are about 50 decibels. A jackhammer is about 100 decibels. Sounds of more than 120 decibels can be bad for your ears. A very loud sound or a bad sound is usually called a noise.

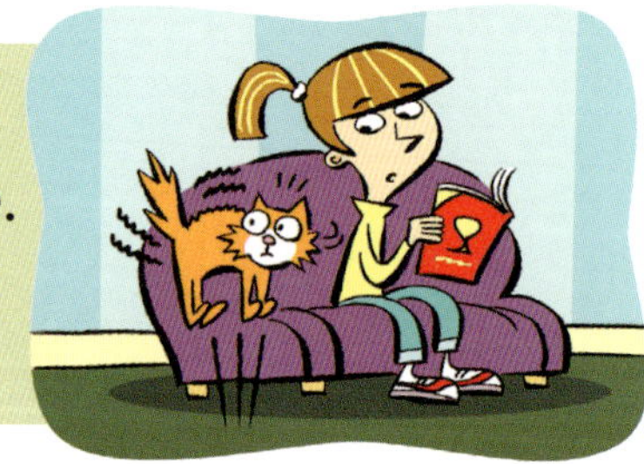

Discover!

Some animals can hear better than people. Your cat can hear more sounds than you!

Don't listen to very loud music with earphones. It can hurt your ears. Other loud noises can be good, like the sound of a car. It tells you, 'A car is coming. Don't cross the street now.' Always listen carefully before you cross the street.

Listen to music, listen to people's voices, listen to the wind. Use your ears and listen to all the sounds around you!

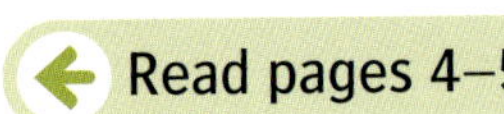 How Sound Moves

← Read pages 4–5.

1 Write the words.

shout   molecule   push
sound waves   voice   ~~waves~~

1 waves

2 __________

3 __________

4 __________

5 __________

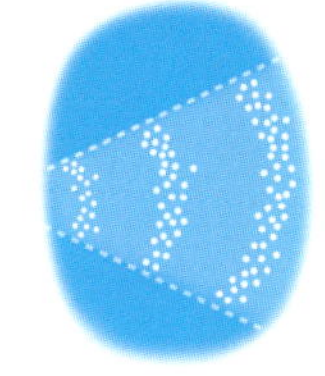

6 __________

2 Complete the sentences.

fast   molecules   move   ~~shout~~   voice   waves

1 When you __shout__ , the sound of your voice moves through the air.

2 Other people can hear the sound of your __________.

3 There are billions of __________ in the air.

4 Molecules __________ like waves in the ocean.

5 Sound __________ are movements of molecules.

6 Sound moves very __________.

3 **Match. Then write the sentences.**

The girl is	the molecules through the air.
Her voice is pushing	moves faster than the bus.
Other people	at 350 meters per second.
Sound moves	shouting.
The sound of a bus	you hear now?
What sounds can	can hear her.

1 The girl is shouting.

2 ______________________________

3 ______________________________

4 ______________________________

5 ______________________________

6 ______________________________

4 **Answer the questions.**

1 Where are you now?

____

2 What sounds can you hear?

____

3 What sounds can you hear when you're in a bus?

____

4 What sounds can you hear when you're in a park?

____

2 Low Sounds, High Sounds

← Read pages 6–7.

1 Complete the sentences.

baby   guitar   truck   high   low

1 A __________ has thin strings and thick strings.

2 The thin strings make a __________ sound.

3 The thick strings make a __________ sound.

4 The sound of a __________ 's cry has a high frequency.

5 The sound of a __________ has a low frequency.

2 Write *true* or *false*.

1 When birds sing, they make a low sound. _false_

2 A guitar has thin strings and thick strings. ______

3 A guitar can make high sounds and low sounds. ______

4 The thin strings of a guitar make a low sound. ______

5 The sound of a truck has a high frequency. ______

6 The sound waves from a truck are thin. ______

3 **Find and write the words.**

1   low   6 ___________

2 ___________   7 ___________

3 ___________   8 ___________

4 ___________   9 ___________

5 ___________   10 ___________

4 **Complete the chart.**

a thin guitar string   a truck   a baby's cry
a bird's song   a plane   a thick guitar string

Things That Make a High Sound	Things That Make a Low Sound
a thin guitar string	

3 Your Voice

← Read pages 8–9.

1 Write the words.

> lungs   chest   mouth
> air   throat   vocal cords

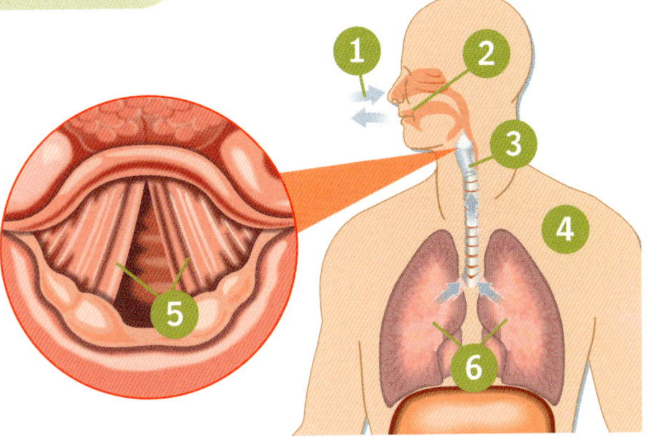

1 _____________

2 _____________

3 _____________

4 _____________

5 _____________

6 _____________

2 Write *higher* or *lower*.

1 A man's voice is ___*lower*___ than a woman's voice.

2 A baby's voice is ___________ than a man's voice.

3 On a guitar, the sound of a thin string is ___________ than the sound of a thick string.

4 The sound of a plane is ___________ than a bird's song.

5 A girl's voice is ___________ than a man's voice.

3 Complete the sentences.

high   longer   mouth   notes   speak   throat

1 Your vocal cords are in your __________ .

2 When you __________ , your vocal cords vibrate.

3 When you sing, you use your __________ , your throat, and your chest.

4 You can make your vocal cords shorter or __________ .

5 Some people can sing __________ notes and low notes.

6 Some people can sing two __________ at the same time.

4 Answer the questions.

1 Where are your vocal cords?

____

2 What do your vocal cords do when you speak?

____

3 Which is usually higher – a man's voice or a woman's voice?

____

4 What can Siberian throat-singers do?

____

4 Musical Instruments

← Read pages 10–11.

1 **Write the words. Then complete the chart.**

> clarinet   cymbals   drum   flute
> guitar   cello   trumpet   violin

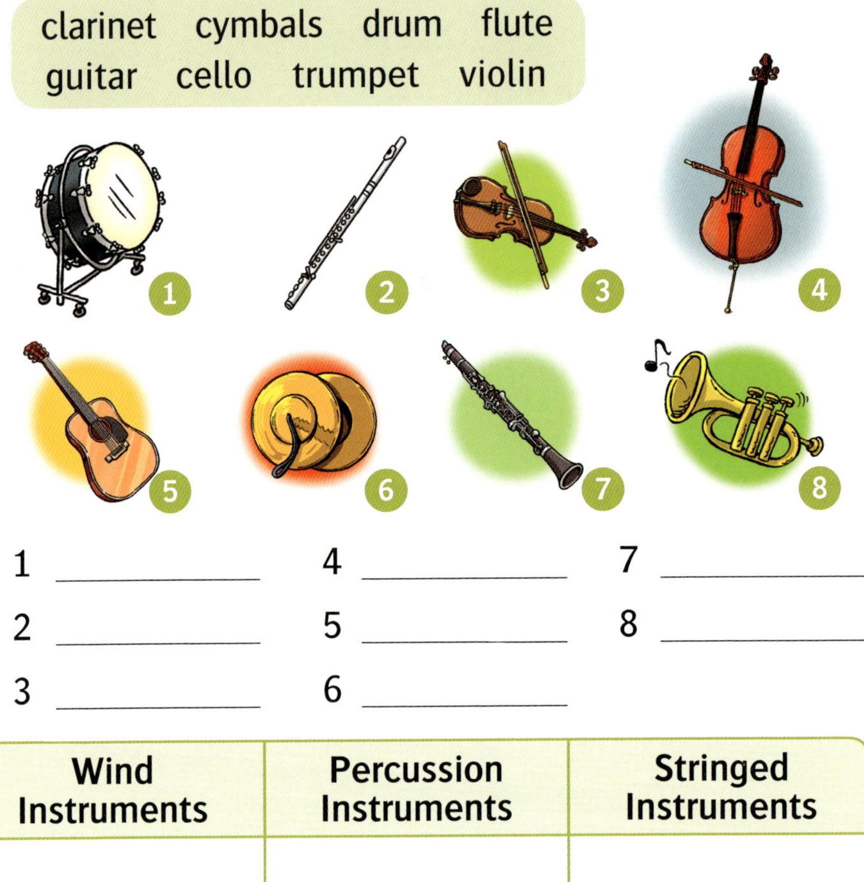

1 _____________   4 _____________   7 _____________

2 _____________   5 _____________   8 _____________

3 _____________   6 _____________

Wind Instruments	Percussion Instruments	Stringed Instruments

2 **Circle the correct words.**

1 Percussion instruments make a sound when the player **hits** / **plucks** them.

2 Xylophones are **wind** / **percussion** instruments.

3 All **stringed** / **wind** instruments have strings.

4 Players pluck the strings or use a **drum** / **bow**.

5 **Cellos** / **Trumpets** and flutes are wind instruments.

6 When the **air** / **voice** in a trumpet vibrates, it makes a sound.

3 **Complete the sentences about you.
Write *can* or *can't*.**

1 I ___________ play the guitar.

2 I ___________ sing.

3 I ___________ play the trumpet.

4 **Write about your friends and family.**

My friend Joe can play the violin.

My friend Serena can't play the guitar.

____

____

____

← Read pages 12–13.

1 Circle the odd one out.

1 sitar (gamelan) bandoneon koto

2 world Japan Argentina India

3 play squeeze floor pluck

4 percussion wind stringed orchestra

5 thirteen two thumb twenty-three

2 Write *true* or *false*.

1 There are only two players in a gamelan. ______

2 There are lots of percussion instruments in a gamelan. ______

3 A bandoneon is like a box. ______

4 You hit a bandoneon to make a sound. ______

5 A koto has three strings. ______

6 Koto players pluck the strings with their thumb and fingers. ______

7 It's easy to play a sitar. ______

8 All sitars have 23 strings. ______

3 **Complete the sentences.**

> floor   notes   orchestras   play   streets   strings

1 People ___________ sitars in India.

2 Some sitars have 23 ___________.

3 In Argentina, people play the bandoneon in
   the ___________.

4 Koto players move the bridges to make
   different ___________.

5 There are ___________ in Bali called gamelans.

6 In a gamelan, the players sit on the ___________.

4 **Match. Then write complete sentences.**

sitar	an orchestra	Indonesia
bandoneon	a stringed instrument	Japan
gamelan	a wind instrument	Argentina
koto	a stringed instrument	India

1 A sitar is a stringed instrument from India.

2 ____

3 ____

4 ____

6 Orchestras and Concerts

Read pages 14–15.

1 Complete the puzzle.

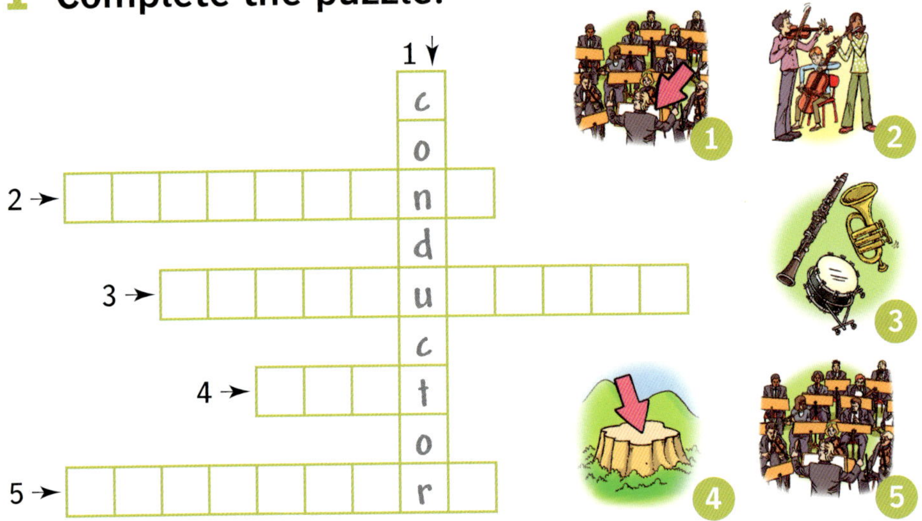

2 Find and write the words.

1 __________   6 __________

2 __________   7 __________

3 __________   8 __________

4 __________   9 __________

5 __________   10 __________

3 Complete the sentences.

> conductor   hall   help
> musicians   practice   walls

1 There are lots of __________ in an orchestra.

2 The musicians always watch the __________ .

3 Conductors move their hands and arms to

  __________ the orchestra.

4 Musicians in an orchestra __________ before
a concert.

5 A big room where concerts happen is called a

concert __________ .

6 The __________ of concert halls are usually made
of different panels.

4 Answer the questions.

1 Who was Wolfgang Amadeus Mozart?

____

2 Where was he from?

____

3 Where is Salzburg?

____

4 Who are the great musicians in your country?

____

(7) Rhythm

← Read pages 16–17.

1 Write *true* or *false*.

1 All music has rhythm. _______

2 All music has the same rhythm. _______

3 The music at rock concerts has
a strong rhythm. _______

4 The rhythm of a marching band
gets faster and slower. _______

5 Flamenco music is from Spain. _______

6 Flamenco music is always slow. _______

2 Match. Then write the sentences.

You tap your foot	is always the same.
There are different	when you listen to music.
The rhythm of a marching band	gets faster and slower.
The rhythm of flamenco music	types of rhythm in music.

1 _______________________________________

2 _______________________________________

3 _______________________________________

4 _______________________________________

3 Order the words.

1 are / There / types / of / rhythm. / different

   There are different types of rhythm.

2 is / strong. / rock / band / The / rhythm / of / a

3 music / Spain. / Flamenco / is / from

4 exciting. / very / is / Flamenco / dancing

4 Answer the questions.

1 What is your favorite song?

2 Can you sing it and tap your foot at the same time?

3 Does it have a strong rhythm?

4 What music has a fast rhythm?

5 What music has a slow rhythm?

← Read pages 18–19.

1 Write the words.

> microphone   sound engineer   MP3 player
> recording studio   musicians   digital signals

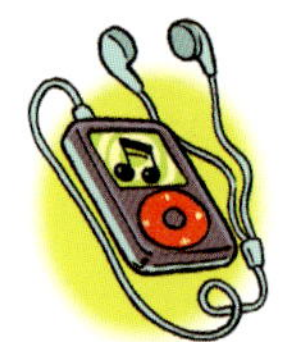

1 ___________

2 ___________

3 ___________

4 ___________

5 ___________

6 ___________

2 Number the sentences in order.

☐ The musicians go to a recording studio.

☐ The musicians play the song in front of a microphone.

☐ Musicians practice the song.

1 A songwriter writes a song.

☐ A sound engineer records the song.

3 **Write correct sentences.**

1 Today, people have MP3 songs.

    Today, people have MP3 players.

2 They can't listen to their MP3 player in the streets.

3 A microphone writes songs.

4 A sound engineer works in a store.

5 A sound engineer doesn't have a computer.

4 **Answer the questions.**

1 Where do people listen to their MP3 player?

2 Where do musicians record their songs?

3 What does a sound engineer do?

4 Do you have an MP3 player?

9 Buying Music

← Read pages 20–21.

1 Write *true* or *false*.

1 People can buy music on the Internet. ________

2 About 100 years ago, people had CDs. ________

3 People had jukeboxes in their homes. ________

4 There were records in jukeboxes. ________

5 People put coins in jukeboxes. ________

6 Cassettes came later than CDs. ________

2 Match. Then write the sentences.

About 100 years ago,
Later, they listened to
Today, people can buy
Compact discs are
Do you

jukeboxes in cafés.
called CDs.
people had record players.
have an MP3 player?
music on the Internet.

1 ____

2 ____

3 ____

4 ____

5 ____

3 Find and write the words.

1 _________   6 _________

2 _________   7 _________

3 _________   8 _________

4 _________   9 _________

5 _________   10 _________

4 Complete the sentences.

CDs   everywhere   home
Internet   player   songs

I like music. There are lots of _________ on my computer. I have an MP3 _________, so I can listen to music _________. When I want to buy a new song, I buy it on the _________. My mother and father have _________. They listen to their CDs at _________ or in the car.

10 Sound and Noise

← Read pages 22–23.

1 Write the words.

> cat   wind   earphones
> car   jackhammer   street

1 ______________

2 ______________

3 ______________

4 ______________

5 ______________

6 ______________

2 Circle the correct words.

1 We **measure** / **hear** sound in decibels.

2 A **jackhammer** / **voice** is about 100 decibels.

3 It's **bad** / **good** to listen to loud music with earphones.

4 Some loud noises can **be** / **is** good.

5 Cats can **see** / **hear** more sounds than people.

3 **Complete the sentences.**

> animals   bad   coming   car   measure   listen

1 We ___________ sound in decibels.

2 Sounds of more than 120 decibels can be

    ___________ for your ears.

3 Some ___________ can hear better than people.

4 The sound of a ___________ can help us.

5 It tells us, 'A car is ___________ .'

6 Always ___________ before you cross the street.

4 **Answer the questions.**

1 How many decibels are people's voices when
   they speak?

  ____

2 Is the sound of a car a quiet sound?

  ____

3 Is the noise of a jackhammer very loud?

  ____

4 Do you like the sound of the wind?

  ____

5 What sounds do you like?

  ____

A Sounds Poster

1 **Make a list of things that make sounds.**

a bird

a radio

a plane

2 **Find photos of these things, or draw pictures.**

3 **Make a poster. Show things that make quiet sounds, loud sounds, or quiet sounds and loud sounds.**

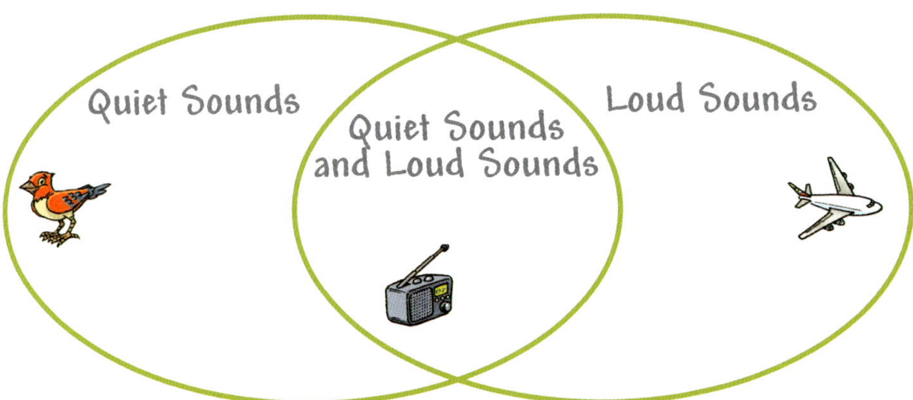

A Music Interview

1 **Interview a friend. Write notes.**

Name: _________________________

1 What type of music do you like?

____

2 Who is your favorite singer?

____

3 What is your favorite song?

____

4 Do you have an MP3 player?

____

5 Do you buy music on the Internet?

____

6 Do you listen to CDs?

____

7 Can you play a musical instrument?

____

2 **Write sentences about your interview.
Display your work.**

Picture Dictionary

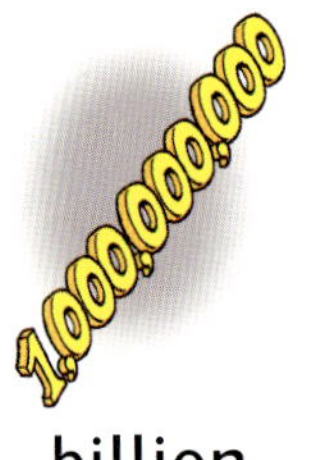
billion

buy

café

coins

cross

cry

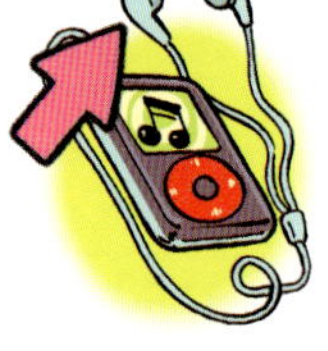
earphones

flat

hurt

lips

loud

man

march

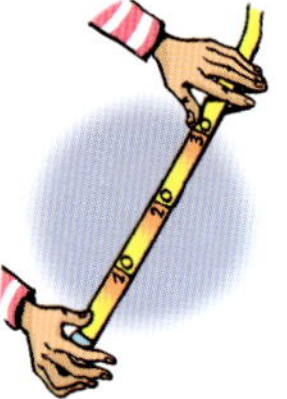
measure

MP3 player

musical instruments

musicians

notes

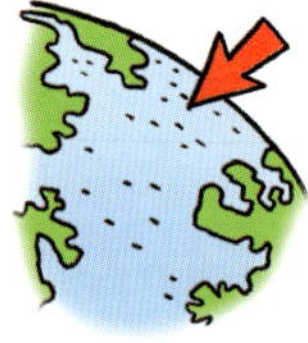
ocean

orchestra

pluck

press

push

quiet

radio

rock band

shout

sound

sound engineer

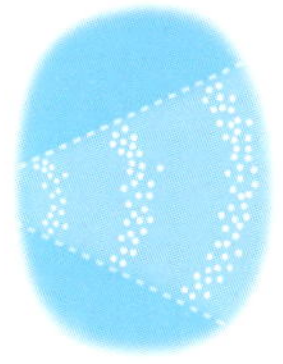

sound waves

squeeze

street

tap your foot

thumb

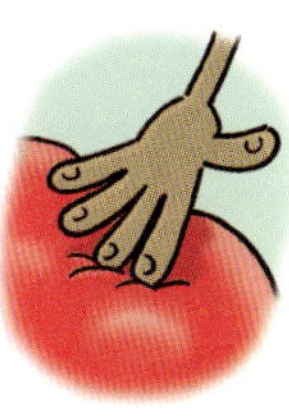

touch

vibrate

voice

waves

woman

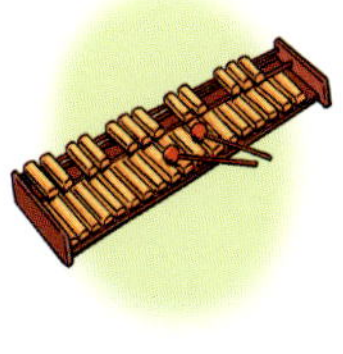

xylophone

Oxford Read and Discover

Series Editor: Hazel Geatches • CLIL Adviser: John Clegg

Oxford Read and Discover graded readers are at four levels, from 3 to 6, suitable for students from age 8 and older. They cover many topics within three subject areas, and can support English across the curriculum, or Content and Language Integrated Learning (CLIL).

Available for each reader:
- Audio CD Pack (book & audio CD)
- Activity Book

For Teacher's Notes & CLIL Guidance go to
www.oup.com/elt/teacher/readanddiscover

Subject Area / Level	The World of Science & Technology	The Natural World	The World of Arts & Social Studies
3 — 600 headwords	• How We Make Products • Sound and Music • Super Structures • Your Five Senses	• Amazing Minibeasts • Animals in the Air • Life in Rainforests • Wonderful Water	• Festivals Around the World • Free Time Around the World
4 — 750 headwords	• All About Plants • How to Stay Healthy • Machines Then and Now • Why We Recycle	• All About Desert Life • All About Ocean Life • Animals at Night • Incredible Earth	• Animals in Art • Wonders of the Past
5 — 900 headwords	• Materials to Products • Medicine Then and Now • Transportation Then and Now • Wild Weather	• All About Islands • Animal Life Cycles • Exploring Our World • Great Migrations	• Homes Around the World • Our World in Art
6 — 1,050 headwords	• Cells and Microbes • Clothes Then and Now • Incredible Energy • Your Amazing Body	• All About Space • Caring for Our Planet • Earth Then and Now • Wonderful Ecosystems	• Helping Around the World • Food Around the World

For younger students, **Dolphin Readers** Levels Starter, 1, and 2 are available.